ESTHER MORGAN

The Wound Register

To Bethany

Very Best Wishes

Esther

30.01.19

BLOODAXE BOOKS

ISBN: 978 1 78037 410 9

First published 2018 by
Bloodaxe Books Ltd,
Eastburn,
South Park,
Hexham,
Northumberland NE46 1BS.

www.bloodaxebooks.com
For further information about Bloodaxe titles
please visit our website or write to
the above address for a catalogue.

Supported using public funding by
ARTS COUNCIL
ENGLAND

Cover design: Neil Astley & Pamela Robertson-Pearce.

Printed in Great Britain by Bell & Bain Limited, Glasgow, Scotland, on
acid-free paper sourced from mills with FSC chain of custody certification.

for Val

ACKNOWLEDGEMENTS

Acknowledgements are due to the editors of the following publications where versions of some of these poems first appeared: *Artemis, The Cortland Review, The High Window, Ploughshares*, and *Writing Motherhood*, ed. Carolyn Jess-Cooke (Seren, 2017).

Special thanks to Moniza Alvi, Andrea Holland and Heidi Williamson who all provided invaluable feedback on draft versions of this collection – their perceptive comments were like a series of light bulbs coming on. Appreciation too, to all the members of the Norwich Stanza group, led by Julia Webb, and to Martin Figura and Helen Ivory for the poetry group they run from their welcoming home. Thank you to Miranda Yates for all her wit and wisdom over (can it be that many years?) – her insights have shaped many of the poems here.

Thank you to my friends and family, especially Kelvyn and Livia. And remembering my grandmother, Elsie Evans, and her father, Frederick Cooper.

CONTENTS

Outbreak

4th August 2014

One hundred years to the day since it started
and I'm sat in the heavy air of the garden
as the monitor flares green with your laboured breathing
wondering where it's all going to end –

my grandmother's grief for her lost father
she carried all her life like a fever in her blood
which shook her and shook her
as the cities are shaken on the news each evening.

Thirteen years since pneumonia hushed her to sleep
only three since they put your seconds-old mouth to my breast
and turned me into a mother, hoping
against hope that love would grant you immunity.

I can still feel the weight of your whole body
as I watch the lights going out house by house
marking something none of us can remember
but which, like the darkness, is being passed on.

1

LATCH

for Livia, b. 12th June 2011

Bobby Shafto's gone to sea
Silver buckles on his knee
He'll come back and marry me
Bonny Bobby Shafto!

ENGLISH FOLK SONG

Latch

I'd assumed it would be effortless –
mid-morning in a park in spring
love laid against me, lightly veiled
with a square of white muslin

not that shove of mouth
to flesh at some ungodly hour
as you struggled to draw milk
threaded red from your ashen mother.

Three weeks and we were done,
my body flowing back into itself
as I waited for the formula to warm
to the same sluggish temperature as blood

the fear revolving in the darkened kitchen
that I would one day fail again
to give you what you needed,
so preoccupied I almost didn't notice

how, ounce by ounce, you put on life
fingers gripping the bottle tightly
while something – rusted shut inside me –
clicked and lifted.

Night Lights

The red shade glows rosily
like a torch shone through flesh and blood

as I watch the gravity with which you feed –
eyes closed, draining the bottle with a slow, tidal suck.

The future shelves steeply away from us
but for now we've electricity, luck.

      Outside the rain's making distances
      passing over our house on its way to the coast

      where a row of lanterns strung out along the shingle
      are night anglers casting their lines into the dark

      and each star shines like a mother on a far-off shore
      holding up her one small light for a signal.

Equinox

(for a nine-month-old daughter)

Somewhere between
the magnolia's poise
and the lit house
where you are sleeping –
arms raised either side of your head
fingers curled as you parachute
through a night sky
cleared now of the day's sharp showers –

I feel the earth's pause:

the tree composing itself like a bride
as she balances her perfect hair
before the service,
before you begin your lifelong tilt
in favour of air, of light
each morning
fresh as white silk
landing you gently a little further away.

At the Checkout

Milk, rice, blueberries, plums –
I'm laying out our weekend along the belt
when the black sack of a storm-cloud splits
with a noise akin to anger or love
and all the mothers look up from the strip-lit aisles
as something larger than ourselves pours down.

I'm frightened says the woman with the mind of a girl,
slipping her carers to come up close and tell me so,
and even though it sounds like the end of the world,
Don't worry, I murmur, *it'll soon be over*

which it is by the time we exit with our load,
the white stones from the opened heavens
heaped and unreal beside the cars,
already melting as I lift each bag into the boot –
the heavy things first, then the things that bruise more easily.

Frozen

At least in this one the love that brings a girl back to life
is a sister's, which makes me feel a whole lot better
allowing you to watch it endlessly, though the dresses
are as pretty as ever, and freedom still seems to mean
letting your blonde hair down and being sexier,
and while it's true the queen gets to build her own castle out of ice,
has her lonely glittering moment on the mountain top
she still has to come back down and make it all ok, thawing the world
with kindness, turning her power into ice rinks for the kids,

though the part you make me play, over and over,
is the scene near the start where I slip
and strike you with a bolt of winter that will mark you forever
and I have to cradle your limp body like a miracle gone wrong
crying *I'm sorry, I'm sorry, I never meant to hurt you.*

Crane

They say a woman climbed one
in her sleep as if
her body understood
our longing to ascend
who – when she woke
to wind singing
through the latticed ribs –
thought she had died
and those cold distances
constituted heaven.

I wonder if you ever
get dizzy looking up
at a future that's always rising
like a skyscraper
glittering and sheer
or if, when your *Mummy, Mummy!*
brings me back to you,
it's anything like that slow swing
through cloudless blue
of a god turning its attention?

In the Wars

Every time I take a swab
of cotton wool and, kneeling,
lift the blood and grit
from your grazed shin
until your sob and shudder eases
and I say *You'll live*
and send you back into the world
to carry on playing

I see the conservator
painstakingly lifting
the layers of yellowing varnish
from the skin of a still-life peach
until it's there before us once again –
startlingly bruise-able and fresh
like everything we handle
when it comes to each other.

Early Years

1 *Winter*

Sometimes when you're not with me
I wish I missed you more.

This morning I handed you over to the girl
who offered you the same sweet smile as all her charges

who led you away along the brightly painted corridor
as you looked back at me roaring No!

> What kind of a mother am I to weigh these words
> against your distress?

> These being all I have to show for the hours I left you
> except for the owl I might have otherwise missed

> gliding silently through the daylight garden
> with her soft feathers and merciless gaze.

2 *Spring*

Outside the star magnolia's swollen buds –
tipped with raindrops from a wintry shower –
have not yet erupted.

Spring is raging in you also,
flushing your cheeks with the need
to bite down hard, as you rock

back and forth on your haunches
like a bear in a zoo, desperate to break
the bars of your own small body.

The bruises are getting ready to bloom
just under your skin, but nothing
is going to stop you from moving,

from wanting whatever is just out of reach –
those strange high shelves where I've hidden away
all our most precious and dangerous things.

3 *Summer*

These evenings I carry your breathing with me
to where the summer peters out

in heaps of old weeds and grass cuttings
and the invisible wire hums through the dusk –

so far and no further.

Out there are the distances I miss:
a late flight banking towards the stars

Doppler shift of cars along the high road
the dark beside the church at the top of the lane.

The monitor glows green like a firefly or planet
marking the border of your dreams

where I stand trying to receive you quietly
the way, sometimes, a poem will begin –

words arriving again like swallows

4 *Autumn*

I'm trying not to make the most of this moment –
a low sun streaming across the garden
the apple tree standing in its halo of windfalls.

I pause – an empty basket at my hip –
between what's been done
what still needs doing.

There will be other evenings, bruised or golden,
sweetness lying where it's fallen in the long grass.
Not everything has to be saved.

Weave

You won't believe in the past:
the rarity of something as simple as an egg,

the Christmas stocking that sounds like a spell –
an orange, a penny, a lump of coal.

No cars, no touch-screens, no *Hello Kitty*,
only the outlandish dark you know from fairytale –

the pretty, hated sister gorging herself sick
on the toy butcher's shop;

the never forgiven baby brother; the wicked mother
rattling her spite like a button tin;

the good father vanished
in a puff of gunfire and smoke

and hunger, whipped like a spinning top,
through every story.

By the time it comes down to you
it will seem like the life of a minor saint,

the girl martyring herself in the backyard dust
turning pebbles and stones into bread.

At school they'll teach you history,
that great, red carpet of royalty and wars

unrolling itself from the looms
which she left school at thirteen to work,

but the past is different,
is what the heart weaves on its own in the night –

a machinery you'd do well to be wary of
with your slight hands, your summer-long hair.

The Wave

You're right to be serious: the white flower
of your hand barely stirring
as the carriages curve out of sight.

Was it me who taught you this gesture,
this hesitant *hello/goodbye* to strangers
for whom – if they chance to look up

from their papers and Kindles,
their rails of boredom and dream –
we are the ones passing?

The moment cools like ironwork or skin,
the cloud shadows moving
like huge airships over the downs.

Timing

Your childhood is pulling away from me
like a bus I'm running flat-out to catch –
unfit as I am –

which refuses to wait, which just
as I think I'm going to make it
is swallowed by the endless river of traffic.

I watch your face pressed against the rear window
mouthing something through the rain-smeared glass,
my chest heaving with jagged breaths

with the kick-myself disbelief that what seemed
like only a minute's inattention – a change of dress,
a mug of coffee misting the garden –

could make this much difference, could leave me
stranded here, fingers still curled
around the one thing I forgot to give you.

One day

if you're blessed with health, if they figure out a way
to stop the war, to keep the rain falling,
I may let you turn into my grandmother

who knew two things at the end of her life –
the brightness of the moon and the taste of water.

You already have her smile – lopsided, hesitant,
the one you use when you think you should be smiling.
The other things will come in time –

the stranger in the night who holds the cup to your lips
the long, white hair I'll brush out for you each morning.

Fog

You love to breathe like this
on the glass of your bedroom window

make the world outside disappear
draw hearts, your name in the mist

turn your mother into a ghost
like a past that's hard to believe in.

> I remember a winter tunnel like this
> kept a degree or two above freezing
>
> light through the polythene – milky, luminous
> like being under someone else's skin
>
> the world outside blurred and hard to believe in
> as a mother through breathed-on glass.

Ahh – the mirror catches my breath
as I feel my bones blurring...

sometimes it's hard to believe I'm a mother
instead of, for instance, that field in the mist

where a girl stands holding her heart like an apple
until something rears out of the whiteness.

Hot House

You step through
a memory of glass
    into pure structure –

a grid of rusted ribs
which holds a grey sky in place.
    This was once an enterprise –

irrigation
    at allotted times
slow release nutrients.

Hard to imagine
    the rainforest heat
like being inside a mouth,

the colours panting –
    scarlet, hot pink, salmon pink,
    burgundy, white

in-between
    the gloved hands
planting and thinning.

Now it's somewhere
    to kick about
on embargoed afternoons

like this –
    far enough from the house
for your mother to have warned you.

Somehow the hours pass
    among the toppled towers
of plastic pots

not happily, exactly,
    but with the absorbed
boredom of moss.

Nothing to speak of
    when you head back
into the lit bustle of tea

nothing to suggest
    that this will be the quiet
that lasts –

unintended, derelict
    coming back at odd moments
to let the rain fall right through you.

Observer's Book

Slowly the blur of green comes into focus:
yarrow, groundsell, common campion, common mallow

their names beginning to dawn on me
the way the first leaves open overnight.

Last week our neighbour died and was buried
in the churchyard – *Gordon Ashfield* –

the first name among the village dead
that I can put a face to –

bending over our broken mower, big hands
winkling the stone out of the blades.

Not that you'll remember him
or stay, as he did, in this one place a lifetime –

like the 'O' in your name which isn't there
I know one morning you'll be gone

each year discarded lightly as a dress
that only lasts a summer.

But for now I want us to belong somewhere,
this place being just as good as any other

and isn't this how it begins –
by naming what is rooted in the earth

as if it's something that you've always known
like my goodnight kiss or the words to *Bobby Shafto*?

Running Wild

(after the photographs of Frances Kearney)

When I tell you *Run along now, be careful*
shrug off my words
like the coat you won't wear to humour me.

As to the deaths you might catch while you're gone –
heaps of collapsible aggregate,
deep pools, sluice gates, weirs,

barbed wire tipped with tetanus,
the boy, damaged and aimless,
with eyes the colour of nightshade –

pay no heed to them.
Read for yourself
the runes of acorn and rainwater,

the scrolls of young fern,
out of range
of all other texts and messages.

And when you return hours later,
self-seeded, hair in rats' tails,
don't tell me a thing,

even if I've the gall to press you.
That silence between us –
that's where you must grow,

the field where the sun
opens and closes its empty pages,
where time runs away with you.

2

FIELD

for my great-grandfather, Frederick George Cooper,
d. 19th July 1916

Twenty men and boys scythed the corn and sang as they went.
'What was the song, Davie?'
'Never mind the song – it was the singing that counted.'

RONALD BLYTHE
Akenfield

Field

A last dog's whistled home
from ground that once
was called after someone:

the common prayer of the wheat,
the hare crouched in her form
among the furrows' sockets of flint,

the rush hour as far away as the river
where that young girl went missing
her night things tumbled over and over.

An acre of average loss
boundaries of parish and family
dissolving in the hiss of this rain:

Lady's Smock, Meadowsweet, Wild Angelica –
the old lace of their names
edging the dark.

Private 2663

In your only photograph
your feet are firmly planted
in their regulation issue
heavy-duty leather,
their blanched tenderness hidden
like something grown underground.

They say some men
walked towards the enemy lines
in a slow-motion trance,
their minds half-shot,
turning the collars of their greatcoats up
as if the bullets were a kind of rain.

Since then you've walked the length of a century
the way a newborn mother,
otherworldly after a sleepless night,
takes each creaking stair –
barefoot and lightly
through the rice-paper quiet.

Charm

I want you to come closer
like the deer that graced my garden one summer
advancing cautiously along the path
its hide flickering in the noonday heat
to almost within reach of my touch.

But you're shy, being dead,
not easily glimpsed or lured
no matter how still I keep, how watchful –
the moon of milk set out on the lawn each evening
still full at dawn.

Perhaps you appear when we're not looking –
untouchable dust
bumping softly all night against the lit glass,
or as thistles in the poorer fields
charming wings and gold out of the air.

Lines of Desire

only the wanting itself persists –
    showing up each summer

      as paler scars in the grass
        cutting the corners

         of recreation grounds and parks
           parting the seas of wheat

           the weight of the heart
            wearing a way

             opening up gaps
              in the hawthorn and gorse

               lighting out
                across the common at dusk

Homo Antecessor

The tide draws a layer of sand back like a cloth
and there they are –
the footprints of our ancestors

sunk into the mudflats of a long-lost river
wandering along the foreshore,
their hunger only an hour old.

The experts deduce five individuals
a mixture of adults and juveniles
heading in a southerly direction

though what the rest of us sees is family:
a mother, a father, daughters, sons,
heel and instep: an impression of tenderness.

In two weeks they're gone again, this time for good
like the last set you made on this earth
ploughed under, along with the bullets and shells,

as my daughter's will be from our walk this morning,
the boot prints she loves to stamp in the mud
filling with rain for the finches to drink from.

Light House

A window shines through the small hours
makes a sea of the surrounding fields.

To the old woman it means someone is dying;
to the homeless, a home;

to the man slipping off his ring before bed
it means someone can't sleep;

to the couple with one empty room
it means a mother is up late nursing her child;

to the mother, a daughter who keeps breaking up
who hasn't returned yet from the Bank Holiday fair;

to the long-haul drivers on their way to the coast
the promise of skin in a different tongue;

and to the woman surprised by brightness next morning
it's almost like love:

the light in the hallway left burning all night
as if the coats and boots had waited up for her.

No Man's

One story survives like the ear's tiniest bone
or a handful of apocryphal verses –

you racing home early from work
knowing only it was serious.

Whether the stone was thrown
or your daughter split her head open falling

whether it was you calling her name
which brought her back to the land of the living

I can't remember, or even if she told me –
like everything else you ever did

or wanted to do, that part is lost.
Who knows, really, what sort of a man you were?

Still I'm touched it's love which raises you up
which sends you running each time out of the mist

your face the one I keep coming round to
swimming towards me through the blood and stars.

Calling

It's as if I've always been calling you
the way those women stood in their doorways
sometimes on summer evenings

calling the names they'd agonised over
trusting they'd carry –
               like owl cries or lowing –

as far as they needed to –
the length of the village then further,
skimming the weir like swallows and into the woods.

And you're here, if you're anywhere
in the gap between love –
               the wheat-field listening with its million ears –

and its answer
galloping out of the dusk, laughing,
mud in her hair, wanting to know what's for supper.

Labours

1 *Planting*

Hawthorn, hazel, hornbeam –
the estate's old retainer

heels them, barely more than twigs,
like crosses into the light sandy soil –

native species deer and rabbit
would strip, come winter,

if it weren't for the spirals of plastic
he slots into place around each one.

So the autumn passes at the same unhurried pace
of a man who knows there's a long way to go,

who seems, by All Souls, to have been here forever –
a figure from a woodcut for a fable

designed to teach our children patience,
to show them what can be accomplished

over time – the thin limbs
stretching behind him in their thousands.

2 *Strimming*

Late spring and the hedgerows surrender
to the machine which moves along these lanes
like time – slow and indiscriminate –
reducing the grasses and wildflowers
to a bleached stubble

like the shaved heads of those poor
requiring correction
who entered the Houses of Industry –
the men through one door
the women and children through another.

3 *Scaring*

Strings of discs with their digital rainbows
ribbons of plastic streaming like high-spirited ponytails
the retort of fake guns, sometimes, still, a home-made man
standing day after day with his arms outstretched
at the centre of a huge loneliness.

This morning a new attempt – the silhouette of a raptor
tethered to the tip of a fifty-foot rod
which plunged and reared in a river of wind
as if an angler had cast his line into the blue
and caught a passing soul –

one of those long gone boys perhaps
paid a few pennies to patrol these acres
flints held tightly in his fists
though it was his heart he hurled each time
the dark thoughts scattering, but never for good.

4 *Harvesting*

By the time the village is stirring
it's over –

the whole hillside shorn of its gold
like something we'd dreamed –

a night machinery working
without terror or dust,

the wheat continuously falling
like a people bowing down.

The stubble looks bluish
in the early morning light.

No need to wake the children yet.
The quiet rises in our houses like bread.

5 *Beating*

A line of men walks slowly across the fields
keeping the same distance apart,
orders passed along the line by a chain of voices.

Keeping the same distance apart
they advance towards the flame-leaved woods,
boots growing huge and heavy with mud.

They advance towards the flame-leaved woods,
their sticks and flags at the ready –
the word travels the line like a lit fuse.

Their sticks and flags at the ready
they start to shout and rattle the trunks
until there's a burst upwards of russet and gold

flushed by the shouting and rattling trunks,
exploding into the open like a sunset.
In the distance the guns start firing

as if the sunset itself were exploding.
The men walk slowly out of the woods.
Soon night will hold them in its soft, black mouth.

6 *Picking*

Each winter they flutter like prayer flags
snagged in the bare branches of trees –

scraps of plastic and rag
remnants of grow bags, torn shirts, dust sheets

gleaming intestines of old cassette tapes,
once a swathe of white polythene

draped like a shroud in the arms of an ash
blown there from who knows where:

ribbons of the thrifty, the wounded, the mad
to be gathered by the old woman

who's made this task her own
singing to herself as she works the hedgerows.

Missing

father   father   father   father
     further and further
you drift
     a word
recited over and over
     until its meaning numbs

     detaches itself
from the once-loved body –
     its wrists and temples –
turning to white noise again
     blurred and flurrying
inside her head –

light as a thistle
     with its fly-away hair –
which bears no relation
     the past dissolving
against her tongue
     like medication or snow

Ovillers, 1919

no crossroads to turn left at
no church to carry on past

no line of poplars along the ridge
to say you're nearly home again

     sometimes when I think of you
     I can almost hear the leaves

     not whispering, the birds
     not singing their invisible territories

Turtil-dove

If I think I glimpse you
wavering at the end of the garden

dressed in its shade like a Sunday suit
how much more elusive is your mother –

an old word fallen out of use
for a bird that was always shy and difficult to spot

even before it was shot each spring
in its hundreds of thousands

trying to make its way back to our vanishing woods
to lay its clutch of small moons

that soft *turr turr* hushing the summers,
another song my daughter will grow up not knowing.

A True and Perfect Inventory

Of all the goods and Chattles
of Henry Monton lately deceased
of the Parish of Salthouse
in the County of Norfolk
being taken the 16th day of July 1729:

In the kitching
one warming pan
one iron pot
one Skillet
one Table

In the Parler or bed house
one bed
& six old Chaires
Two smale puter dishes
and six old plates

In the Chamber
one bed

Two small cows
and two Buds and one pig
A small Cart
Three small old Horses

Lumber and things forgot

Stories

A quiet man's bone-crushing handshake; Trev's dog
turning up days later on the GPO steps, literally knackered;
inedible sponge cakes that *wouldn't even bloody burn*;
the whole pub hushing as she gave them a tune;
the cars that free-wheeled home on booze and petrol fumes;
the good-time guy larking about on top of the carriage
with the tunnel coming – all of them scattering
like sticks of gum flung from the GI jeeps

or that red-jacketed monkey escaped from the docks
who went chattering over the roofs of the back-to-backs –
Aunty Val, a slip of a girl, in hot pursuit
along with what seemed like the whole of Newport
everyone ducking the tiles and laughing their heads off
as they chased him along the street and into legend.

Naming a Star

It feels like the right gift for you –
your scattered ashes gathered at last
to a single pin-point
in all that bright field

and instead of a cross
an unknown woman bringing the washing in at dusk
who tilts the pale dish of her face to the sky

the faint light of your dying
still travelling towards her.

Register

The old village school order
white-sleeved and obedient –

Attoe, Bird, Bird, Butcher
Coddling, Dobbie, Edmunds, Fairhead

Fiske, Garrould, Gillingwater, Gorbel
Gray, Hale, Hamilton, Hansy

Johnson, Kent, Norman, Prior
Reynolds, Rodwell, Runicles, Sampson,

Seeley, Simmons, Smith, Strowger,
Williams, Williams

– the snowdrops in the churchyard
answering *Here! Here! Here!*

Browsing

Time was, the rings of flesh
which mushroomed overnight in the darker grass
were said to be the dreams of village girls

pushing upwards through the flinty soil,
capped and delicate, from a place
they knew deep down but couldn't name

which is the past's unrecoverable shade
where cows are always lying beneath the elms
replete with their body's one desire

and the word *cloud* has only to do
with the changing weather or the snowy
sunlit place where God still lives

from whom no secrets are hid
as if anything so timeless ever existed
(voices murmuring in church like bees in the lilac.)

Though now our screens glow every night
luminous as the fields of rape
each bait taken, each message thread

uploaded to endless acres of machines
where history's encoded, link by link,
we might be forgiven for wanting to go back

to a time when memory was loving and then over
and our names could be divested of their lives
left behind like piles of clothes along the river.

At the Thiepval Memorial
19th July 2016

1 *Cooper, F. G.*

It's like scouring a dictionary for the right definition,
our eyes travelling up and down the columns
of hand-carved names until they light on yours
with its ghost of an ancestor

who knew how to shape each stave of oak
using tools he could have handled in his sleep –
adze, broadax, compass, drawknife, plane –

until the segments came together sweetly
like a flower closing in the evening garden.

2 *Cornfield, H.*

And then, four deaths below your own,
a space opens up, golden and swaying,
somewhere I might lay to rest
the little I've gleaned of you –

a handful of facts scattered like ashes
at the edges of an older meaning,
its usage rare now, almost as obsolete

as the men who sang through the falling corn
their wives and daughters following behind them.

Pastime

If it's true our spirits survive
for as long as anyone utters our name,

a kind of recalling
that keeps on hauling us back to this world

perhaps I should hold a service of forgetting
towards the end of a hot summer's day

pausing half-way across a set-aside field
to let the coastal wind whistle through me

while your great, great-granddaughter passes the time
stripping seeds from the flowering grasses.

3

RESTORATION

for my grandmother, Elsie Evans, née Cooper,
b. 22nd October 1906, d. 17th January 2001

The glacier knocks in the cupboard,
The desert sighs in the bed,
And the crack in the tea-cup opens
A lane to the land of the dead.

W.H. AUDEN

Smithereens

a bowl, a plate
the blue, glass bauble
I told her not to touch

how the lightest tap
    (an egg at the edge
    of a mixing bowl

    someone breaking
    the news
    about your father)

is all it can take –
the world
splintering outwards

every part

speeding further away

from   every   other   part

      *

Here's a piece –
your daughter's grip
on the steering wheel
knuckles whitening

and here –
the same hands cupping
the blown bulb
of your skull

and here –
a splinter lodged
in the corner of my eye
in the fear

here –
where the pale star
shines on her cheek
from the time

I let her run
with a too-sharp stick
and here – right down
to my fingertips

the skin
at her temples
(here –
where the bone

is thinnest)
so soft
it almost
doesn't exist

Bonding

I tried to hold you together
when I was little –
you who taught me how to whip tops, roller-skate
who bought me bags of soft, pink rock from the market each week,
the Tiny Tears I pestered for one birthday,
fed me home-grown raspberries with top of the milk.
You called me *My Sweet*
damned, in the same breath,
the Ities, the Labourites, your mother, your brothers and sisters,
made rules you shaped your life to,
entrenched positions:
No Visitors Except Family, No Visiting,
No Forgiveness of Trespasses –
lines of fault and blame you bore to your grave.

Lines of fault and blame you bore to your grave:
No Forgiveness of Trespasses,
No Visitors Except Family, No Visiting.
Entrenched positions
made rules you shaped your life to:
the Ities, the Labourites, your mother, your brothers and sisters
damned in the same breath
you called me *My Sweet*.
You who fed me home-grown raspberries with top of the milk,
who bought me the Tiny Tears I pestered for one birthday,
bags of soft, pink rock from the market each week,
who taught me how to whip tops, roller-skate.
When I was little
I tried to hold you together.

Mending

I know what my daughter's carrying in her cupped palms
by the way she crosses the lawn towards me
as if it might still be broken or spilt
as if I'll know what to do with it.

I dig a small hole at the back of the flowerbed
and she watches closely as I bury her faith
in me to mend anything, while the apple blossom
eddies down like a ripped-up picture.

When I was little you brought me
not your father, but his loss – slack and warm
in your hands as a freshly shot rabbit.
We laid it across our laps and stroked it together.

Fragments

nests of white china
kept for best
in the high cupboards

their untouched rims
and gold circles

one minute he was there
the next –

your great-granddaughter's
picking over the furrows
at the field's edge

the loveliest bits
are shaped, identifiable –

the curved lip
of a jug

a glazed handle
scrolled and delicate
as an ear

in the car
they chink and chatter
in their plastic ice-cream tub

at home, tipped out
they bring back kitchens
their unforgiving slates

and blackened ranges
women kneeling
at a loss

they bring back your hands
careless
in the early light

the cup they are ferrying
into the ever-after

Somme

shadow
    on the lung
of your summers

closer to bomb
    than home

closer to sob
    than song:

a constant hum
    on your tongue,
in your bones

the marriage of sound
    and sense:

the French for men,
    the English for gone

the sum of all loss
    the taking away from:

your father
    The Son

the sodden ground
    of your grief

beneath
    its sump
in the soil

above
     the sombre drum
of the rain

the swung bronze
     of its name

taking its lifelong
     toll.

Blood

isn't really anything like poppies –
the bright splashes I opened the door to that day
closer to ink from a shaken nib,
the fingerprints smeared on the jambs
more like a crime scene than petals;
nothing ornamental or wild about the spotted hankies
the soaked dishcloths and towels
strewn around that shambles of a kitchen
where nothing like birth or death had taken place,
no carnage, no blow to the face,
just something, thinned with age, beginning to flow
that could not be staunched or appeased
that left you standing, bathed red and swaying
in the wind that swept over you.

Redcurrants

Glamorous dangling strands
like the kind of earrings
you'd never be seen dead in;

a glut of flesh each summer
coaxed from your garden's
unpromising soil,

handed over to your daughter
by the bucket-load
to do something with.

It took a patient violence
stripping each string
through a fork's gritted teeth

hours of simmering,
an avalanche of sugar
to combat the bitterness

though in the process
something was clarified –
a past which set like the evening sun

which slid,
seedless and pure,
over our tongues' horizon.

Conservation

You kept what was left of him
sealed and dustless:

his archived face blurred
beneath sheets of acid-free paper;

the Book of Hours you shared on this earth
hidden behind a black velvet cloth;

the pinned moths of goodnight kisses
inside the summer dusk of a sliding drawer;

his touch like a fern in the rare herbarium
its fingers splayed against the page.

Even your voice donned special white gloves
when you spoke to me about him

turning his love in the darkened hush
like the last known egg of its kind.

The Doll

I used to think this story meant your father,
finery handed down to you one Christmas from on high,
given a few weeks later to a baby brother
too sickly to know what he wants

except it isn't this hard, painted face thrust into his own
by a woman elbow-deep in worry and six kids' washing
who reaches for whatever comes to hand,
anything to make the screaming stop.

But since I've learned to heed that cry
any hour of the day or night
I think what you were trying to tell me
was not a metaphor for death but life,

how when you've been given what you've always dreamed of
it's bound to come to grief sooner or later,
broken on some ordinary morning
by a mother who doesn't even notice what she's done.

The Casualty Book

Each soldier's meticulously inked
against his given pain –

Gun Shot Wound, Gas Poisoning, Fever,
Frost-bite, Dysentery, NYD

(Not Yet Diagnosed) Shell-shock.
Though what remains unregistered

are the wounds for which no names exist –
the silence of returning men

carrying what was left of their lives
the way the lad caught up in his first engagement

picked an arm out of the mud
unsure if it belonged to him or not;

and the deaths, beyond words, of the missing
which can only be entered in our dreams

*(his skin smoothing over at your touch
like a page before the place and date of writing.)*

Celadon

You dreamed of your father after rain
of a sky fired to the precise blue-green

the Emperor of the Northern Song
glimpsed in a dream seven centuries before.

Some days the sky clears to the colour
of that heaven you tried hard to believe in

luminous as the glaze of the vase
his courtiers brought him before he died.

He thought he was dreaming when he opened
his eyes, that he was back in that dream

where the sky cleared after all-day rain
leaving him walking alone in the silk orchard.

        Before my daughter was born, it stopped raining:
        in the sun the cabbage field broke

        into thousands of white wings
        fluttering up from the furled blue-green hearts.

Restoration

In Imperial Japan
the craftsmen repaired

the fractures brought to them
with veins of gold

as if the damage
is what makes things precious –

small comfort to the girl
whose problem isn't

that her heart is broken
but that it keeps on beating

grief pounding away –
its muscle memory.

                    *

It's not my place
to make everything perfect

though when it comes to you
I have some sympathy

for those healers of antiquities
working late into the lighter evenings

as they pieced together
arms, legs, torsos, heads

for the streams of Grand Tour wealthy
who wanted their heroes good as new:

a kind of lying
bordering on love.

*

Perhaps this is the closest we can come
to that older meaning –

the living at work
in the christening rain

re-opening trenches in the earth
patiently retrieving, bone by bone,

those green recruits
of Le Bois Faison –

each one given back
his missing name

their deaths handed out
like letters from home.

*

A bowl of thin air –
the guessed curve of a life:

your father cupping
the peach-fuzz weight

of his daughter's head
as he lowers you – slowly now –

into your dreams
like a gloved curator

angling a piece of rare dynasty
into a case: fluted, translucent,

the soft plates
not yet knitted together.

I hope it wasn't

the light's
efficient mercy
which called you
but blackbirds
singing deliriously
demobbed from winter
in Brinton's Park
a stranger
brushing the dirt
from his knees
as he breaks off
from his work
lifting and splitting
the summer lilies
as the girl is lifted
onto Daddy's shoulders
(*sometimes she pretends*
to be tired so he will
have to carry her home)
then saying your name
like an old variety
grown for its sweetness
in south-facing gardens
and you feel yourself
sheltered, unsealing
the blurred features
of loved ones
leaning towards you
drinking you in

In the Night Garden

The sky clears after day-long rain
to an evening chilly and pure as a snowdrop.
A low sun glitters the washing line

like that necklace which came apart in your fingers
the glass beads stuttering across the kitchen tiles
like teeth in a dream.

I should call you in –
your favourite programme's about to start –
the stars are already bursting into blossom,

the cheery characters, eager to please,
are bouncing up and down
in their padded, harmless bodies

but I'm still on my hands and knees
trying to retrieve from these scattered moments
the facet and shine of our lives together

and you are still busy with your latest ritual
crouched in the day's extra minute of light
their pale heads nodding as you sing to them.